This book belongs to

_____

_____

and I am finding out
about the story
of Christmas

It's that wonderful time of year.
December has arrived –
and all the joys of Christmas.

As Christmas day gets nearer,
we buy our Christmas tree,
we put up decorations,
we send cards, we sing carols,
and we act in nativity plays.

We buy presents for our friends
and our family – and hope
Father Christmas will visit us too!

But what's the real meaning of Christmas?
This little booklet retells the story
of the very first Christmas
– and why it still matters for us.

Would you like to know
The Story of
Christmas?

by Tim Dowley
Illustrated by Eira Reeves

CANDLE
BOOKS

A young woman named Mary lived in the little town of Nazareth.

One day the angel Gabriel appeared to her.
"You are going to have a very special baby!"
said the angel. "You must call him Jesus."

Mary was amazed – and a little bit frightened.
"I will do whatever God wants," she said.
The angel left her.

Mary loved a carpenter named Joseph.
Mary and Joseph got married straight away.

It was nearly time for Mary's baby
to be born.

But Joseph and Mary had to travel to Joseph's home town, Bethlehem. It was a long, tiring journey.

At last they arrived.
Joseph asked at the inn,
"Please, do you have a room?"

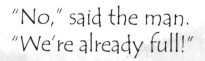

"No," said the man.
"We're already full!"

"But I have a stable where the animals sleep,"
he added kindly. "You're welcome to that!"

There, among the donkeys and cows,
Mary's precious baby was born.

Joseph laid soft straw in the animals' feed box. Baby Jesus soon fell asleep there.

In fields outside Bethlehem, the sky lit up.
"It's an angel!" said a frightened shepherd.

"Don't be afraid!" said the angel. "I have great news. Christ the Lord is born as a baby in Bethlehem. Go and see!"

Then crowds of angels filled the sky. They sang, "Glory to God – and peace to people on earth!"

When the angels had all gone,
the shepherds ran to Bethlehem
to search for the baby.

They soon found the stable.
The shepherds knelt before baby Jesus.

At about the same time, wise men in
a far country saw a special star in the sky.

"That means a new king has been born," they agreed.

So the wise men followed the star
all the way to Bethlehem.

There it stopped, right over the place
where Jesus was.

The wise men knelt before little Jesus.
They had found the new king!
They gave Jesus precious presents:
gold, and rich perfumes
called frankincense and myrrh.

At Christmas time we give presents too.

And we remember that at the first Christmas Jesus was born in Bethlehem.

Christmas is the time when we celebrate
the birth of baby Jesus, God's own Son.

Shepherds, wise men, and angels
all visited when baby Jesus was born.
They knew he was no ordinary baby.
He was specially sent by God to save us.